Money is Trust

Bob Seeman

ISBN: 9798863731209 (Hardcover)
ISBN: 9798863731377 (Paperback)

Cover design by: CyberCurb

Publisher: CyberCurb, Vancouver

Money is Trust

About the Author

Bob Seeman is the Managing Partner of CyberCurb and a Mentor at the Rogers Cybersecure Catalyst and Techstars. He helps technology entrepreneurs make the complex simple.

Bob also has published *Brevity, Reward Risk, Artificial Intelligentsia, Power in Mistake, On Trust, How Business Decisions Really Get Made, The Cybersecurity Handbook,* and *The Coinmen.*

He is a California attorney, electrical engineer, and board director. Bob is a co-founder and former director of RIWI Corp., a public company that conducts data analytics, and has advised governments internationally on technology and business issues. Previously, he was Head of Strategy for Microsoft Network in London, and a technical consultant to the European Commission.

Bob previously practiced administrative law with an international law firm. He holds a Bachelor of Applied Science (Elec. Eng.) with Honours from the University of Toronto, a Master of Business Administration from EDHEC, and a Juris Doctor (J.D.) from the University of British Columbia.

For my wife

Table of Contents

Money is Trust

Bob Seeman

"I will tell you the secret to getting rich on Wall Street. You try to be greedy when others are fearful. And you try to be fearful when others are greedy."

"It takes 20 years to build a reputation and five minutes to ruin it."

Warren Buffett

Warren Buffett is an American billionaire business magnate. He has been called an "oracle" of smart investment. His advice: Buy low, sell high. Easy to say. Hard to do.

"Our economy is based on spending billions to persuade people that happiness is buying things, and then insisting that the only way to have a viable economy is to make things for people to buy so they'll have jobs and get enough money to buy things."

Philip Slater

Philip Slater was an American sociologist. He also wrote novels and plays. He is best known for *The Pursuit of Loneliness*, which argues that most of us are unhappy no matter how affluent we are, because we are too greedy.

"If we didn't have greed, market economies wouldn't be as innovative as they are. But in my view, greed has to be contained by the fear of losses, so there has to be a system where, if you take too much risk, you go into bankruptcy. You don't systematically bail out people who take excessive risks."

Nouriel Roubini

Nouriel Roubini is an Iranian-American economist. He was an early critic of cryptocurrencies which he viewed as catering to greed.

"I think greed is a terrible thing unless you are in on the ground floor."

"A nickel ain't worth a dime anymore."

Yogi Berra

Yogi Berra gained fame as a baseball coach known for his witty one liners. They're funny precisely because they're contradictory.

"Capitalism is the extraordinary belief that the nastiest of men for the nastiest of motives will somehow work together for the benefit of all."

"The importance of money flows from it being a link between the present and the future."

John Maynard Keynes

John Maynard Keynes was a British economist who believed that governments should often intervene to make sure that the greed of the nasty men was kept in check.

"The problem of social organization is how to set up an arrangement under which greed will do the least harm. Capitalism is that kind of a system."

"Well first of all, tell me: Is there some society you know that doesn't run on greed? You think Russia doesn't run on greed? You think China doesn't run on greed? What is greed? Of course, none of us are greedy, it's only the other fellow who's greedy. The world runs on individuals pursuing their separate interests. The great achievements of civilization have not come from government bureaus. Einstein didn't construct his theory under order from a bureaucrat. Henry Ford didn't revolutionize the automobile industry that way. In the only cases in which the masses have escaped from the kind of grinding poverty you're talking about, the only cases in recorded history, are where they have had capitalism and largely free trade. If you want to know where the masses are worse off, worst off, it's exactly in the kinds of societies that depart from that. So that the record of history is absolutely crystal clear, that there is no alternative

way so far discovered of improving the lot of the ordinary people that can hold a candle to the productive activities that are unleashed by the free-enterprise system."

Milton Friedman

Milton Friedman was a very influential American economist who received the Nobel Prize in Economics in 1976. His position was that greed fuels capitalism and free trade and is, therefore, to be championed.

"It's true: greed has had a very bad press. I frankly don't see anything wrong with greed. I think that the people who are always attacking greed would be more consistent with their position if they refused their next salary increase. I don't see even the most Left-Wing scholar in this country scornfully burning his salary check.

Greed will continue until the Garden of Eden arrives, when everything is superabundant, and we don't have to worry about economics at all."

Murray N. Rothbard

Murray Newton Rothbard was an American libertarian economist. The word greed conjures up the image of Scrooge from Charles Dickens' A Christmas Carol. Scrooge is a cold-hearted miser who despises Christmas. However, by the end of the story, Scrooge sees the error of his ways, and he becomes a better, more generous man, using his wealth to help others.

"To borrow against the trust someone has placed in you costs nothing at first. You get away with it, you take a little more and a little more until there is no more to draw on. Oddly, your hands should be full with all that taking but when you open them there's nothing there."

Jeanette Winterson

Withdrawals from the Bank of Trust: People will trust you at first, but not for long if you don't produce.

"Trust, but verify."

Ronald Reagan

The words are a trusted and true Russian proverb: "Доверяй, но проверяй".

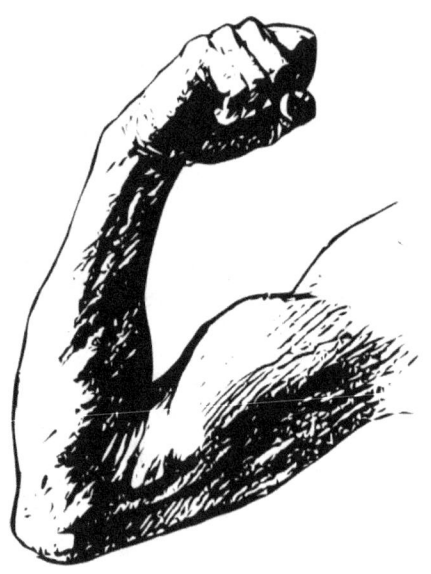

"In God we trust, all others pay cash."

Jean Shepherd

"Where large sums of money are concerned, it is advisable to trust nobody."

Agatha Christie

"The primary reason people believe in anything is because others believe."

Brian Norgard

"Too many people spend money they earned to buy things they don't want to impress people that they don't like."

Will Rogers

"Every day is a bank account, and time is our currency. No one is rich, no one is poor, we've got 24 hours each."

Christopher Rice

"What we really want to do is what we are really meant to do. When we do what we are meant to do, money comes to us, doors open for us, we feel useful, and the work we do feels like play to us."

Julia Cameron

"Money never made a man happy yet, nor will it. The more a man has, the more he wants. Instead of filling a vacuum, it makes one."

Benjamin Franklin

"Many people take no care of their money till they come nearly to the end of it, and others do just the same with their time."

Johann Wolfgang von Goethe

"Formal education will make you a living; self-education will make you a fortune."

Jim Rohn

"Happiness is not in the mere possession of money; it lies in the joy of achievement, in the thrill of creative effort."

Franklin D. Roosevelt

*"If all the economists were laid end to end,
they'd never reach a conclusion."*

George Bernard Shaw

"Every time you borrow money, you're robbing your future self."

Nathan W. Morris

"Not everything that can be counted counts, and not everything that counts can be counted."

Albert Einstein

"When I was young, I thought that money was the most important thing in life; now that I am old, I know that it is."

Oscar Wilde

"A bank is a place where they lend you an umbrella in fair weather and ask for it back when it begins to rain."

Robert Frost

"A bank is a place that will lend you money if you can prove that you don't need it."

Bob Hope

*"Money can't buy love, but it improves
your bargaining position."*

Christopher Marlowe

"That money talks, I'll not deny, I heard it once: It said, 'Goodbye'."

Richard Armour

*"I've got all the money I'll ever need,
if I die by four o'clock."*

Henny Youngman

"Anybody who thinks money will make you happy, hasn't got money."

David Geffen

"So you think that money is the root of all evil. Have you ever asked what is the root of all money?"

Ayn Rand

"The problem with socialism is that you eventually run out of other peoples' money."

Margaret Thatcher

"A fool and his money are soon elected."

Will Rogers

"Most people work just hard enough not to get fired and get paid just enough money not to quit."

George Carlin

"Money is power, and in that government which pays all the public officers of the states will all political power be substantially concentrated."

Andrew Jackson

"Work is that which you dislike doing but perform for the sake of external rewards. At school, this takes the form of grades. In society, it means money, status, privilege."

Abraham Maslow

"You aren't wealthy until you have something money can't buy."

Garth Brooks

"I made my money by selling too soon."

Bernard Baruch

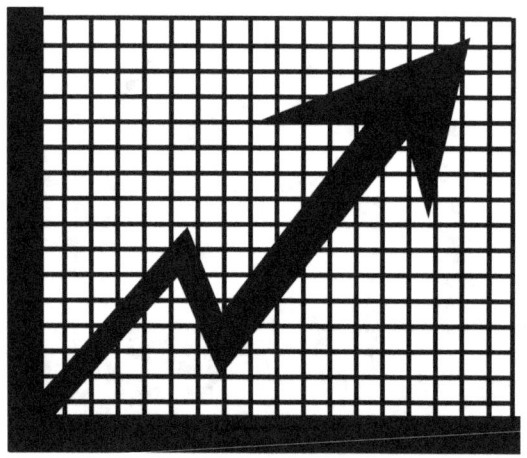

"The Seven Social Sins are:

Wealth without work.
Pleasure without conscience.
Knowledge without character.
Commerce without morality.
Science without humanity.
Worship without sacrifice.
Politics without principle."

Frederick Lewis Donaldson

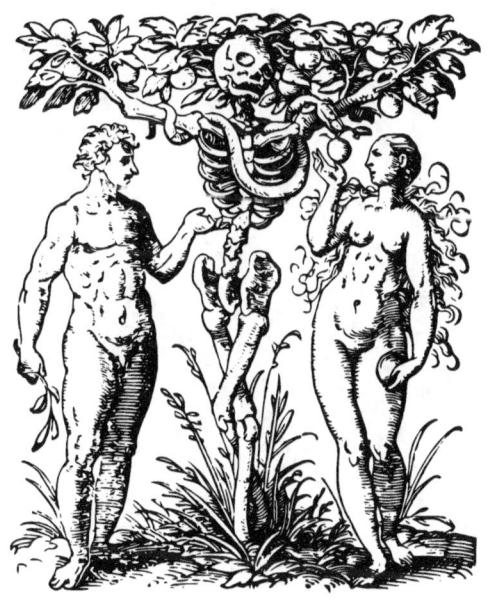

"If you think nobody cares whether you're alive, try missing a couple of payments."

Anonymous

*"If all the nations in the world are in debt,
where did all the money go?"*

Steven Wright

*"If you lend someone $20, and never see
that person again; it was probably
worth it."*

Anonymous

*"(Starbucks) doesn't have a slogan yet, so I
thought of one for them...
'It's really expensive, but the
line is long.'"*

Karen Bergreen

*"In spite of the cost of living,
it's still popular."*

Kathleen Norris

"The easiest way for your children to learn about money is for you not to have any."

Katharine Whitehorn

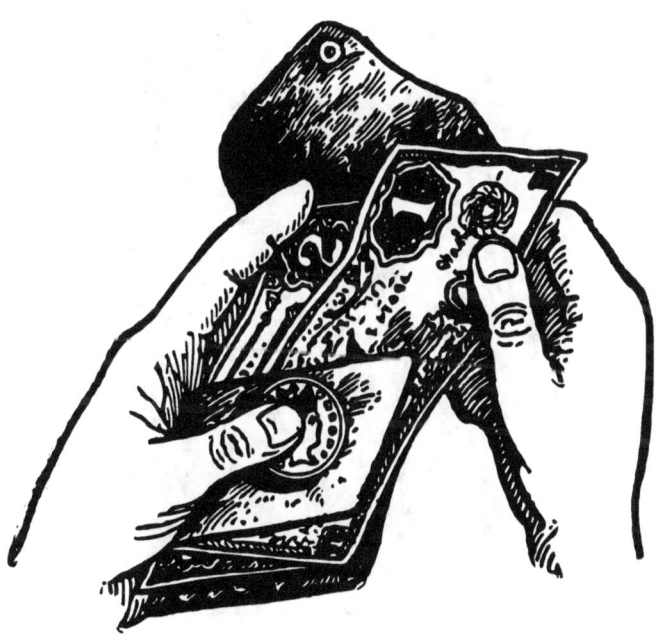

"The poor wish to be rich, the rich wish to be happy, the happy wish to be married, the married wish to be dead."

Ann Landers

"When you get something for nothing, you just haven't been billed for it yet."

Franklin Jones

"There's a way of transferring funds that is even faster than electronic banking; it's called marriage."

Sam Kinison

"I think it's wrong that only one company makes the game Monopoly®."

Steven Wright

"While money can't buy happiness, it certainly lets you choose your own form of misery."

Groucho Marx

"If you owe the bank $100, that's your problem. If you owe the bank $100 million, that's the bank's problem."

J. Paul Getty

"If only God would give me some clear sign! Like making a large deposit in my name at a Swiss bank."

Woody Allen

"I don't have a bank account because I don't know my mother's maiden name."

Paula Poundstone

Bob Seeman

"Anytime four New Yorkers get into a cab together without arguing, a bank robbery has just taken place."

Johnny Carson

"Trust is the lubrication that makes it possible for organizations to work."

Warren Bennis

"Trust is an important lubricant of a social system. It is extremely efficient; it saves a lot of trouble to have a fair degree of reliance on other people's word. Unfortunately this is not a commodity which can be bought very easily. If you have to buy it, you already have some doubts about what you have bought."

Kenneth Arrow

"It is mutual trust, even more than mutual interest, that holds human associations together."

H. L. Mencken

"If there is one trait that your brand must speak of, it is trust."

Idowu Koyenikan

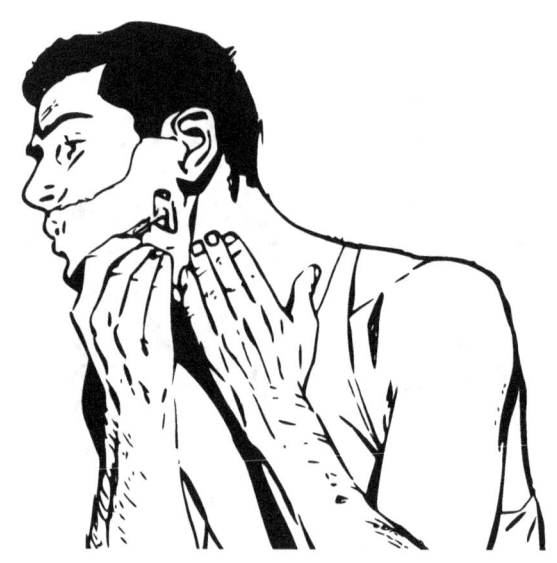

"Trust everybody – but cut the cards."

Finley Peter Dunne

A thief stuck a pistol in a man's ribs and said, "Give me your money."

The man, shocked by the sudden attack, said: "You cannot do this, I'm a United States congressman!"

The thief said, "In that case, give me my money!"

Mugging

Sign of the times

"To this day, the boy that used to bully me at school still takes my lunch money.

On the plus side, he makes great Subway® sandwiches."

Lunch money

"I asked God for money

I later found out that God doesn't work that way.

So I robbed a bank, then asked for forgiveness."

Confession of sins

"Two reasons I don't give money to homeless people:

1. They would spend it on alcohol.

2. I want to spend it on alcohol."

Money for alcohol

Q: Where do atheists donate their money?

A: Non Prophet organizations

A donation to a large non-profit

"I'm so good with managing money.

I got a letter from a credit card debt
collector saying 'outstanding payment'."

Credit Card Bill

This is a bill in which you have to pay. If you do not pay within one (1) month, a $250.00 fine is assessed.

Name: John Phillips
Address 123 Main Street
San Francisco, CA 12345

Phone: (123) 456-7890
CC Number: XXXXXXXXXXXX1234
Bill Received: 01/16/1968

Your Transactions

Item	Price
The ABC Store - Cookies	$2.81
Orville's Bakery - Donuts	$5.95
Stan's Gas Station - 10 Gallons of Gas	$40.00
	Total: $48.76

Credit card debt

The widow of an African dictator was found dead with $45 million cash under her bed.

She had spent the last 10 years trying to share it, but no one replied to her emails.

Giving it all away

When Putin began his first term in office in 1999, he asked the then outgoing president Boris Yeltsin if he had any advice for him since he, Putin, had no prior experience in politics.

Yeltsin handed him two envelopes and said, if things go bad, open the first envelope. If things go extremely bad, open the second envelope.

Putin put the envelopes in his bottom drawer.

In 1999 till early 2000, things got really bad. The central bank had defaulted and the effects were felt everywhere. Unemployment was rife, stores were empty and people were in the streets hungry, angry and protesting.

In desperation, Putin reached for the bottom drawer and pulled out the first envelope. In a small note, it was typewritten "Blame your predecessor."

Putin blamed Boris Yeltsin, his predecessor, for the woes of Russia, the dissolution of the Soviet Union as the biggest disaster in its history and told his compatriots to give him time and power and he would make Russia great again.

It is now 2023, with the central bank at near default, people protesting in the streets, economy in shambles, and a war that isn't going well.

Putin reaches for the second envelope in the bottom drawer. In it he reads a typewritten note with the message, "Prepare two envelopes."

Two envelopes

A German walks into a bar and orders a beer.

The bartender tells him: "20 euros."

The German is shocked, "20 euros? Yesterday it was only 3 euros!"

"Well, today it is 20 euros."

"But why 20, damn it?"

Bar tender: "I'll explain it. 3 euros is beer, 3 euros to help Ukraine, 4 euros assistance to European countries who have imposed sanctions and are not members of the EU, and 4 euros in aid to the UK, for successful implementation of sanctions against Russia. Then, 3 euros are sent to the Balkan countries as aid to buy furnace coal, and, finally, 3 euros for a gas subsidy for the EU and fund to help maintain sanctions."

The German silently gave the bartender a 20 euro note. The bartender took it, put it in the cash register and gave him 3 euros back.

The German, in disbelief, asked, "Wait, you said 20 euros, right? I gave you 20, why are you giving me back 3 euros?"

"We have no beer."

Beer

"I went the ATM to take some cash out,
and selected the option
"Cash with Advice".

It said "Get a better job."'

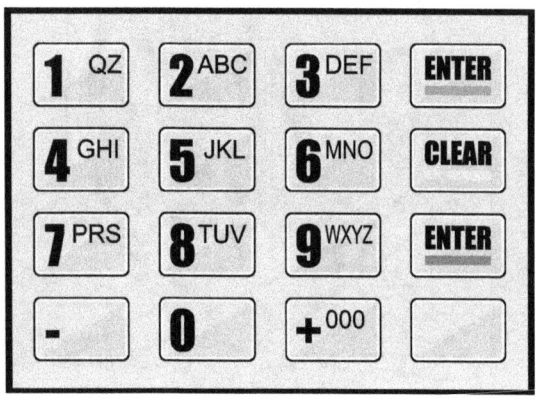

ATMs